CW00858839

BUGS

From bumblebees to dung beetles,
explore the creepy-crawly world of insects

Contents

LITTLE TIGER
LONDON

CATERPILLAR BOOKS
An imprint of the Little Tiger Group
www.littletiger.co.uk
1 Coda Studios, 189 Munster Road, London SW6 6AW
Imported into the EEA by Penguin Random House Ireland,
Morrison Chambers, 32 Nassau Street, Dublin DO2 YH68
First published in Great Britain 2022
Text by Noodle Fuel 2022
Illustrations by Rich Watson 2022

A CIP catalogue record of this book is available from the British Library
ISBN: 978-1-83891-456-1 • CPB/2800/2080/1121
10 9 8 7 6 5 4 3 2 1

This means that we're dealing with a very big number indeed!

Wherever you see this symbol, you can be sure that this is a record-breaking fact!

And these facts will absolutely burst your brain!

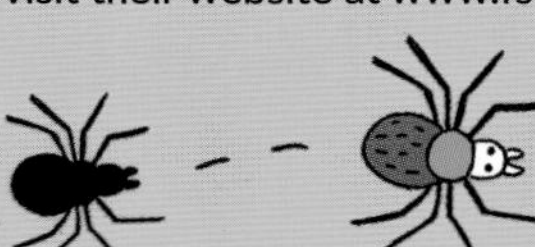
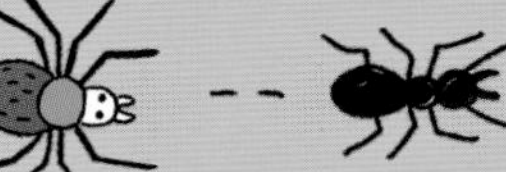

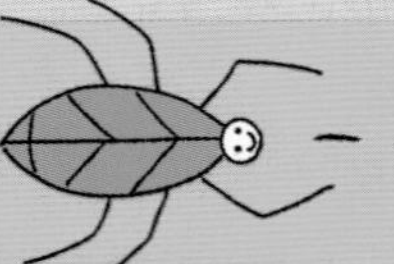

Welcome to the weird and wonderful world of BUGS!

Insects make up nearly **three quarters of all animal species** on Earth.

There are a lot more of them than there are of us!

Their bodies have **three** sections.

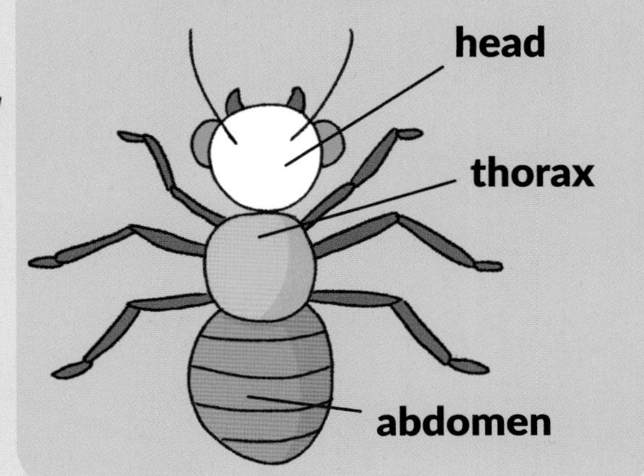

Most insects belong to **just six** main groups:

- Beetles
- Bees and wasps
- Bugs
- Butterflies and moths
- Crickets, grasshoppers and locusts
- Flies

Insects have **six** legs.

It's a good job they don't wear shoes!

We are including spiders in our creepy-crawly tour, even though technically they aren't insects! Check out page 32 for more info!

All insects have a tough outer shell – this is called an **exoskeleton**.

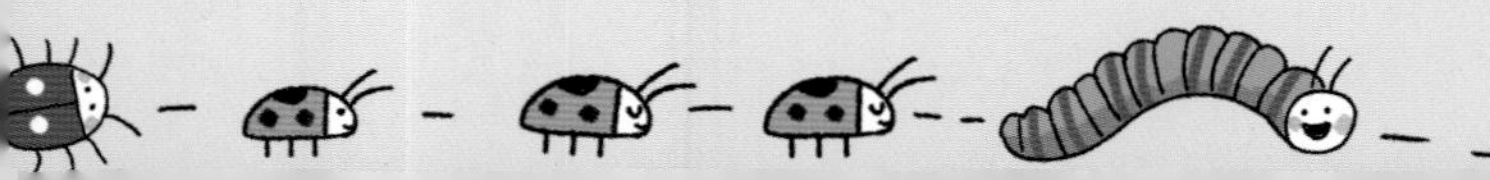

Most insects follow a four-stage life cycle.

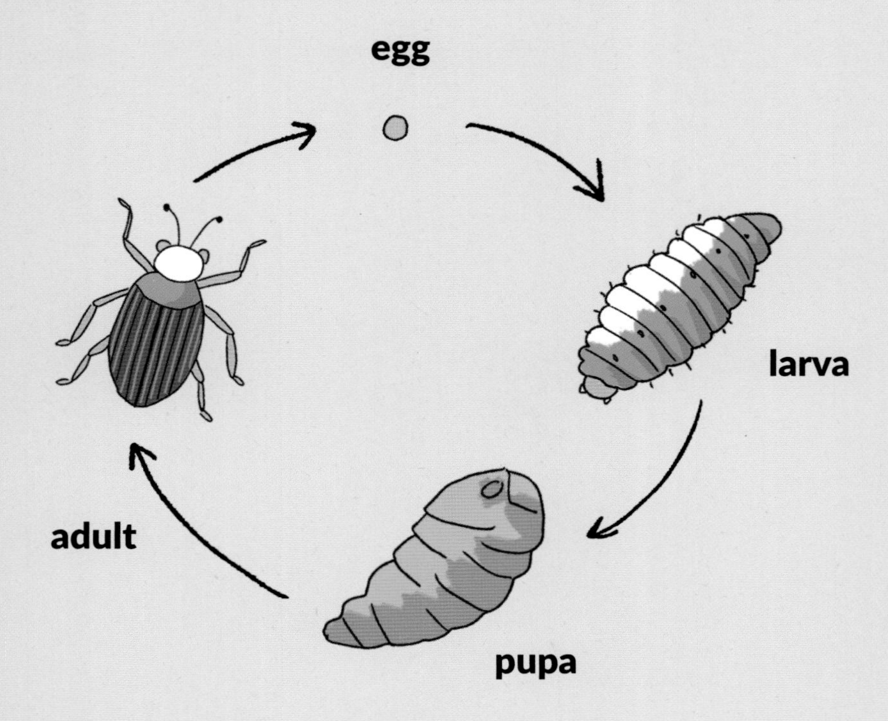

Bugs can be found everywhere, but there is **only one insect** that is native to Antarctica – the *Belgica antarctica*, a tiny midge that can't fly.

They must get very cold feet!

Insects eat lots of different things and each species has **evolved** to eat a certain type of food.

You don't want to know what some of them eat...

Insects are **important** in nature. They have many roles, but their main job is to break down dead material.

Insects normally have two **antennae** – these are used for sensing their surroundings.

It is impossible to count the number of insects on Earth, but it could be as many as **ten quintillion**.

That's 10,000,000,000,000,000,000.

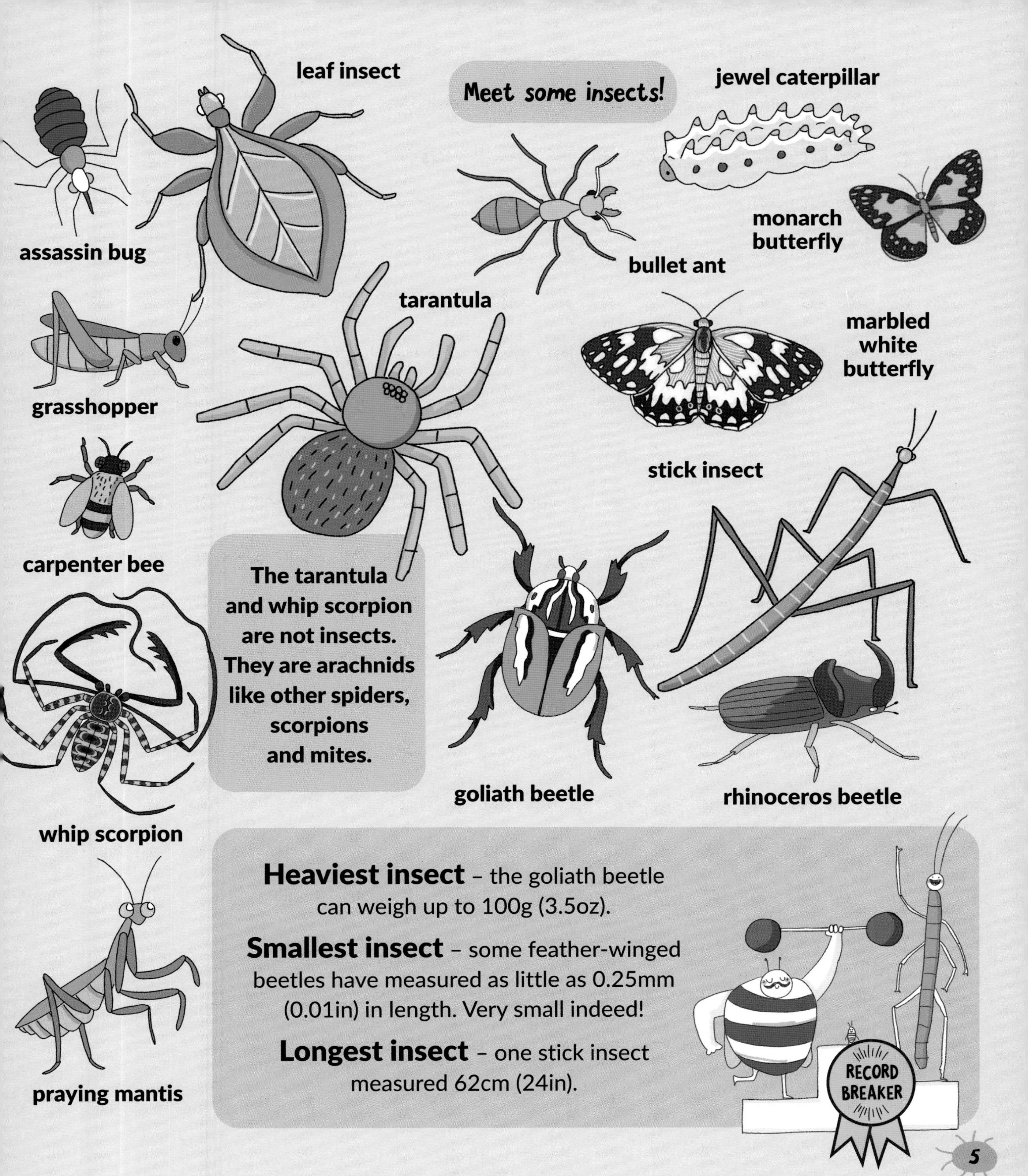

Heaviest insect – the goliath beetle can weigh up to 100g (3.5oz).

Smallest insect – some feather-winged beetles have measured as little as 0.25mm (0.01in) in length. Very small indeed!

Longest insect – one stick insect measured 62cm (24in).

Bees

Bees are important for pollinating flowers, which helps the flowers reproduce. Without bees, many plants could not grow at all.

A honeybee hive is a series of combs formed from **six-sided cells** made of wax.

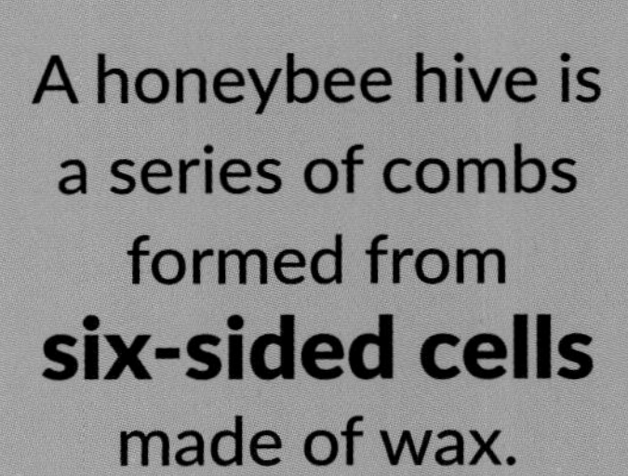

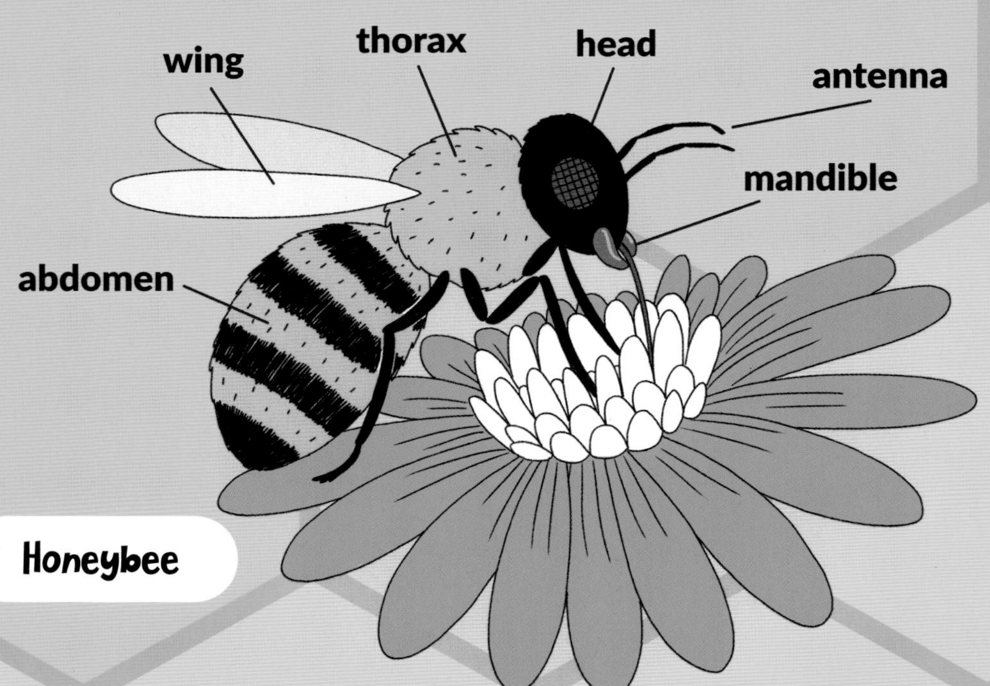

On average, a honeybee queen can lay **1,500 eggs** per day.

Honeybees communicate with each other by **doing a little dance**.

The world's biggest bee is as long as a person's thumb and has a **wingspan of 6.5cm** (2.6in) – the species is called Wallace's giant bee.

RECORD BREAKER

You're safe with male bees as **only female** bees sting.

Unfortunately, checking is difficult and a very good way to get stung!

Bees have been found on **every continent** except Antarctica.

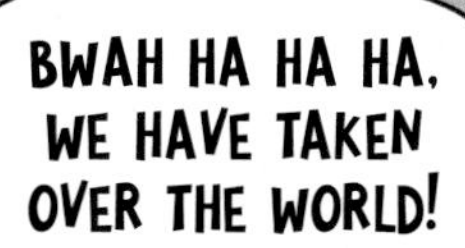

One bee will, on average, only create one twelfth of a teaspoon of **honey** in its life.

Just think how much work must go into a whole jar!

Bumblebees can sting many times, but honeybees **die** after they sting.

All worker bees are **female**. Male bees, or drones, only exist to mate with the queen.

The buzzing sound of a bee comes from its **wings**, as they flap at great speed.

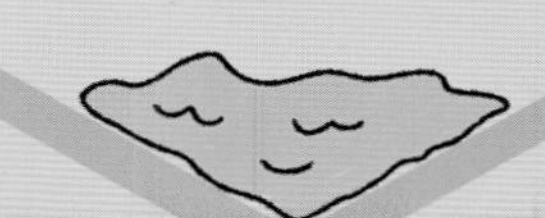

Fireflies

Fireflies glow in order to attract **mates** and potentially to discourage predators.

Fireflies live as larvae for up to two years before pupating. As adults, they live just long enough to mate and lay eggs – usually less than a month.

Some fireflies **don't eat anything** during their short adult lives. However, certain hungry females do use special flashing patterns to lure in males that they then eat!

Firefly larvae are good hunters. They track slugs and snails using their slime trails and then **paralyse and eat them**.

We're *not* sure we want to go on a firefly larvae picnic...

Firefly

antenna

head

mouth part

leg

wing

A firefly glows by taking in oxygen and adding it to a special substance called luciferin inside its body. The two chemicals mix to produce light.

It's not just the adult fireflies that like to put on a show; **firefly eggs** glow too!

It's because they run on el-egg-tricity!

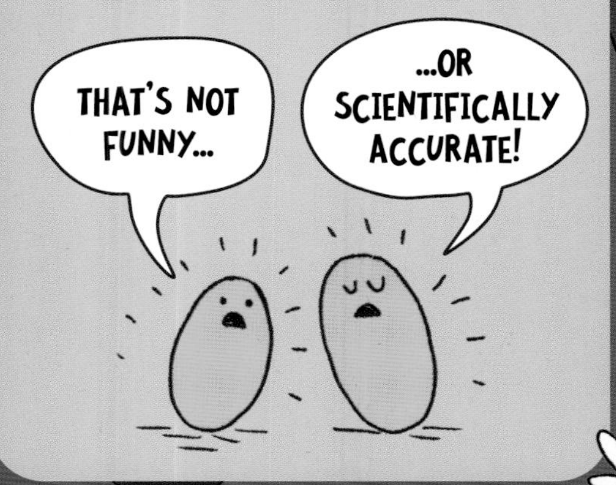

When a male firefly is looking for a mate, it will often flash in **special patterns** that are unique to its sub-species.

The firefly is not really a fly at all; it's actually a type of **beetle**.

Frogs prey on fireflies, and sometimes they eat so many that they start to **light up**!

Not all fireflies glow. Certain sub-species are active during the day and use **scent trails** to find a mate instead.

When frightened, fireflies shed tiny drops of their own blood that taste bitter and are **poisonous to many animals**. This defence mechanism is known as reflex bleeding.

Flies

Flies use just **one pair of wings** for flying. The second pair is used to maintain balance.

Flies may sometimes be pests, but they also serve an important role as **plant pollinators** in areas where there are fewer bees.

There are about **125,000** species of flies.

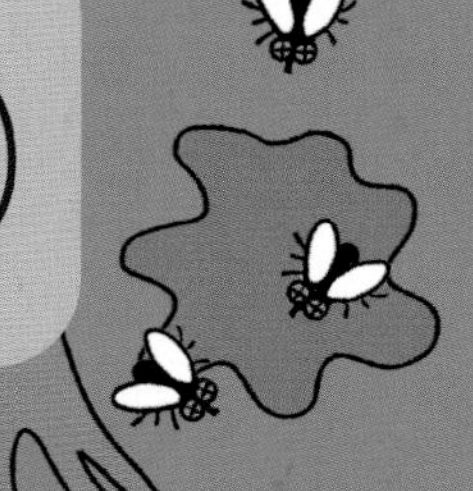

It is thought that the housefly and blowfly together carry **600 kinds of infection**.

To flies, humans seem to move in **slow motion**, which is why flies are so hard to catch.

Houseflies will lay their eggs on items such as **poo, rotten meat and decaying fruit**. This gives their baby maggots something to eat when they're born.

Now, how does that sound as a first meal? Yuck!

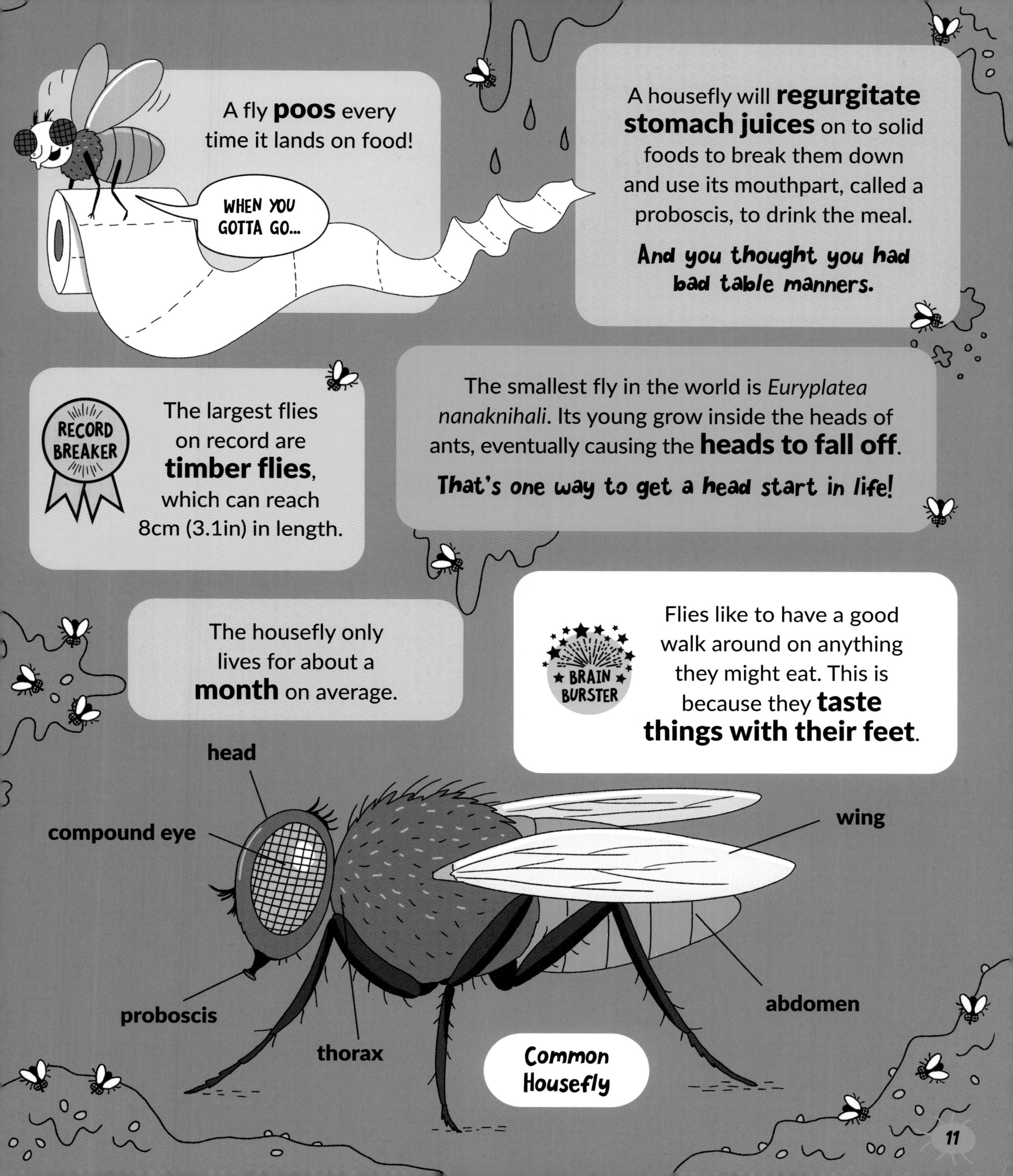
A fly poos every time it lands on food!
WHEN YOU GOTTA GO...
A housefly will regurgitate stomach juices on to solid foods to break them down and use its mouthpart, called a proboscis, to drink the meal.
And you thought you had bad table manners.
RECORD BREAKER
The largest flies on record are timber flies, which can reach 8cm (3.1in) in length.
The smallest fly in the world is Euryplatea nanaknihali. Its young grow inside the heads of ants, eventually causing the heads to fall off.
That's one way to get a head start in life!
The housefly only lives for about a month on average.
BRAIN BURSTER
Flies like to have a good walk around on anything they might eat. This is because they taste things with their feet.
head
compound eye
proboscis
thorax
wing
abdomen
Common Housefly
11

Mosquitoes

There are estimated to be **one hundred trillion** mosquitoes around the world.

Mosquitoes live near water sources such as **swamps and ponds**, due to the important role water plays in their life cycle.

Smelly feet are attractive to some species of mosquito!

Only the female mosquito sucks blood. Male mosquitoes are **vegetarians**!

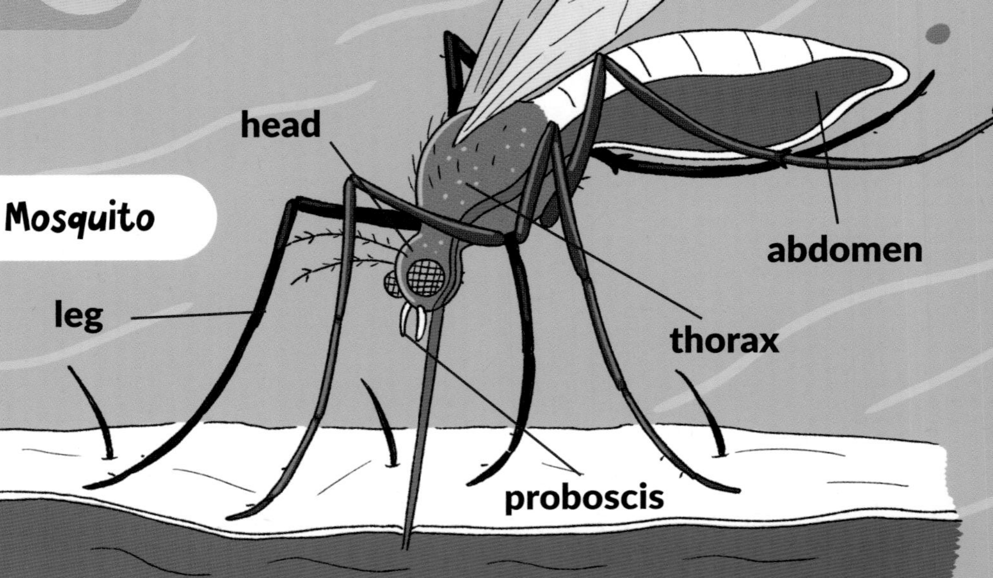

Mosquitoes are an important part of the **food chain**, providing food for other animals such as birds, frogs and fish.

Due to the **nasty diseases** that they carry, mosquitoes are responsible for the deaths of more people than any other animal.

Mosquitoes are attracted to the gas carbon dioxide, which is unfortunately why they are also attracted to **human breath**.

If your breath smells of feet, you're really in trouble!

A female mosquito can consume **up to three times** her own body weight in blood.

I THINK I MAY HAVE OVEREATEN!

Mosquitoes have been around since the **Triassic period** – that's 251 million years ago.

Nature's little vampires are much more active during a **full moon**!

I WANT TO SUCK YOUR BLOOD!

BUZZ OFF!

Ladybirds

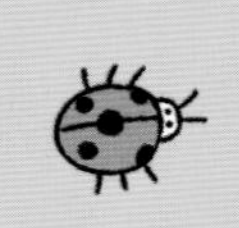
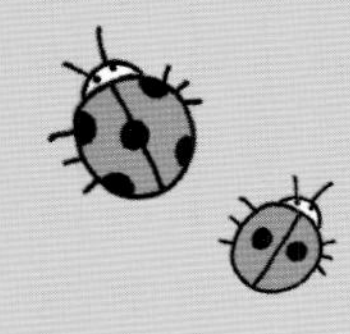

Ladybirds can **fly at 60kmph** (37mph) and at heights of 1.1km (3,600ft).

Ladybirds, also known as **ladybugs**, are a type of beetle.

Ladybirds can have **red, yellow or black** shells.

Ladybirds use their bright colours to confuse predators. If that doesn't work, they secrete a **smelly fluid** and play dead.

Ladybirds are vulnerable to predators as they're usually spotted...

A ladybird has two pairs of wings. The outer pair forms a hard, protective layer, and the inner pair is used for flight.

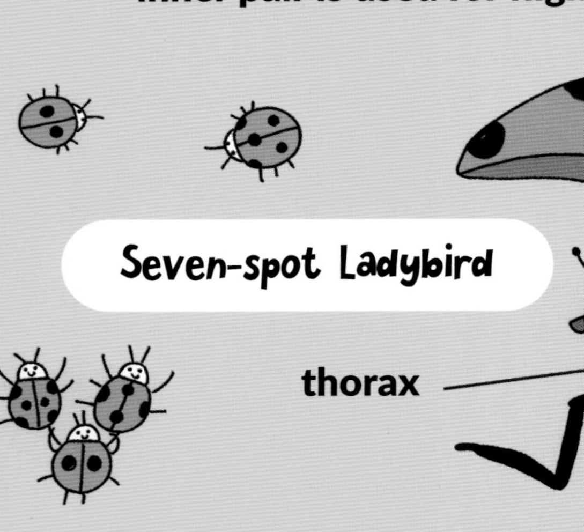

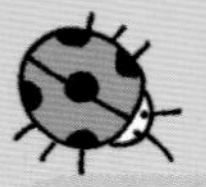
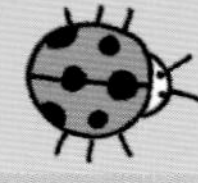
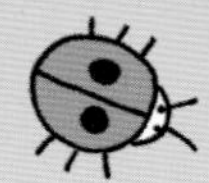
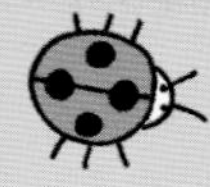

Ladybirds may look cute, but if they get hungry enough they'll **eat each other**!

Ladybirds are useful to farmers as they eat some crop pests. One ladybird alone can eat **5,000 aphids** in its lifetime.

That's quite an appetite for a tiny bug!

Adult ladybirds **hibernate** over the winter.

They live **all over the world**, except in Antarctica and the far northern regions of North America, Europe and Asia.

They're not big fans of the cold.

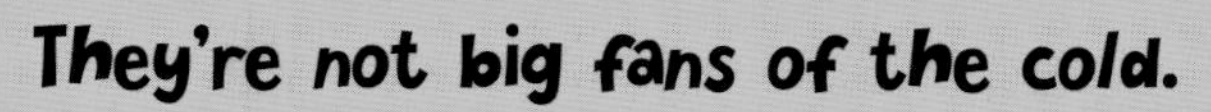

Ladybirds are considered symbols of **good fortune** around the world and it is thought to be bad luck to kill them!

Ladybirds prefer to live where there are **lots of plants**, such as gardens, fields and woodland.

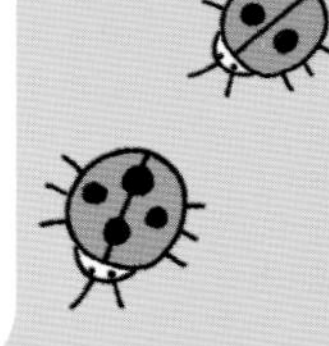

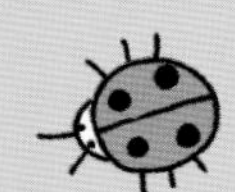
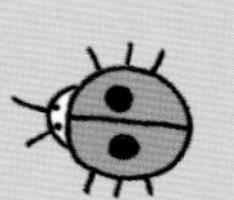

Caterpillars and Butterflies

A caterpillar may grow to be **one hundred times** the size that it was when it hatched.

The Butterfly Life Cycle

egg

caterpillar

chrysalis

butterfly

Caterpillars eat so much and grow so fast that they may need to **shed their skin** up to five times.

Caterpillars love eating leaves. This is good for their development but makes them a **pest** for farmers and gardeners.

marbled white

swallowtail

Caterpillars have **six sets** of eyes, but can only sense light rather than seeing clear images like we do.

malachite

monarch

red admiral

large white

peacock

Monarch butterflies migrate distances greater than **3,000km** (1,800mi). They breed in the north-east United States and then travel south to Mexico.

That's a big journey for little wings!

The largest butterfly in the world is the Queen Alexandra's birdwing butterfly, which has a **wingspan of up to 28cm** (11in).

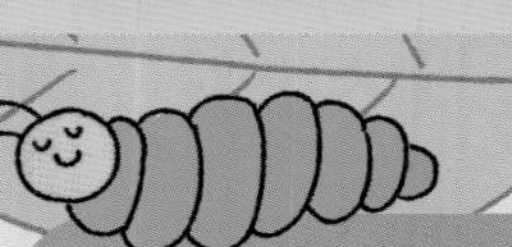

There are around **17,500** species of butterfly in the world.

Butterflies have some of the best natural **camouflage** in the insect kingdom.

BUTTERWHO?

Grasshoppers and Crickets

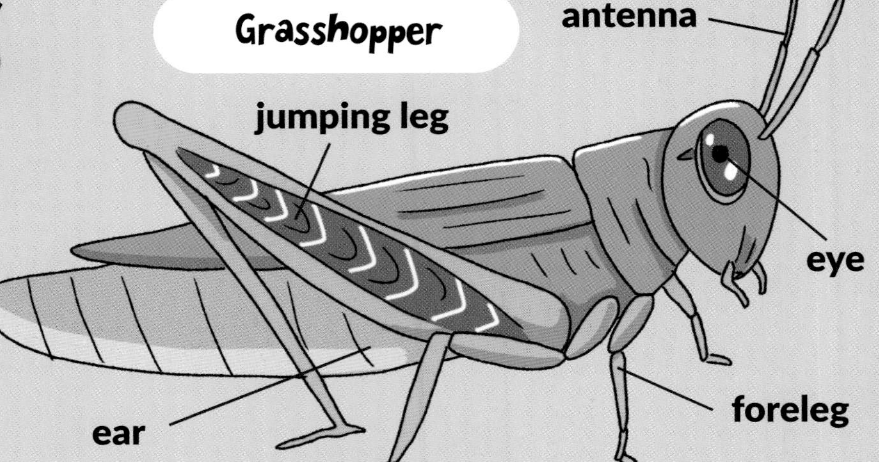

Crickets and grasshoppers make their **distinctive sounds** by rubbing their legs or their wings together.

The simplest way to tell the difference between a cricket and a grasshopper is that a cricket has **longer antennae**.

They're also better at tap dancing, but they keep that to themselves!

Some grasshoppers can jump almost **1m** (3ft) in a single bound.

That's the same as a person being able to jump the length of a basketball court.

China has an **ancient custom** of valuing crickets. They are kept as pets, symbolising luck, and people even hold cricket fights!

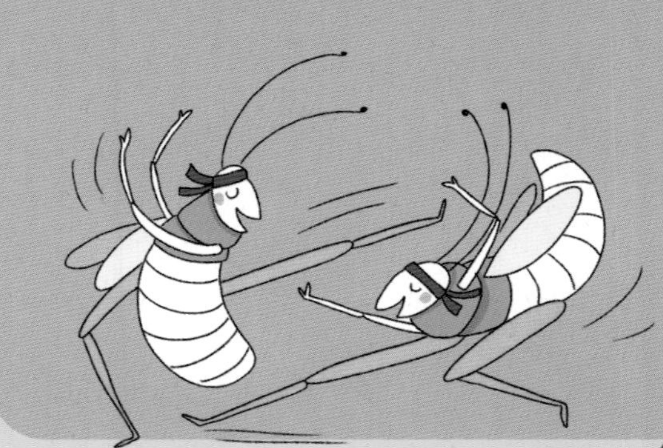

A cricket's **ears** are on its legs.

A grasshopper's ears are on its **abdomen**.

You can roughly estimate the temperature in Fahrenheit outside by **counting** the number of times a cricket chirps in 15 seconds and adding 37.

You can also check if they're wearing a woolly hat, scarf and gloves.

Crickets make their familiar noise to **attract mates**, but it also puts them at risk from predators.

There are over **25,000** types of grasshoppers and crickets.

The camel cricket earned its name from its humped back!

Dragonflies and Damselflies

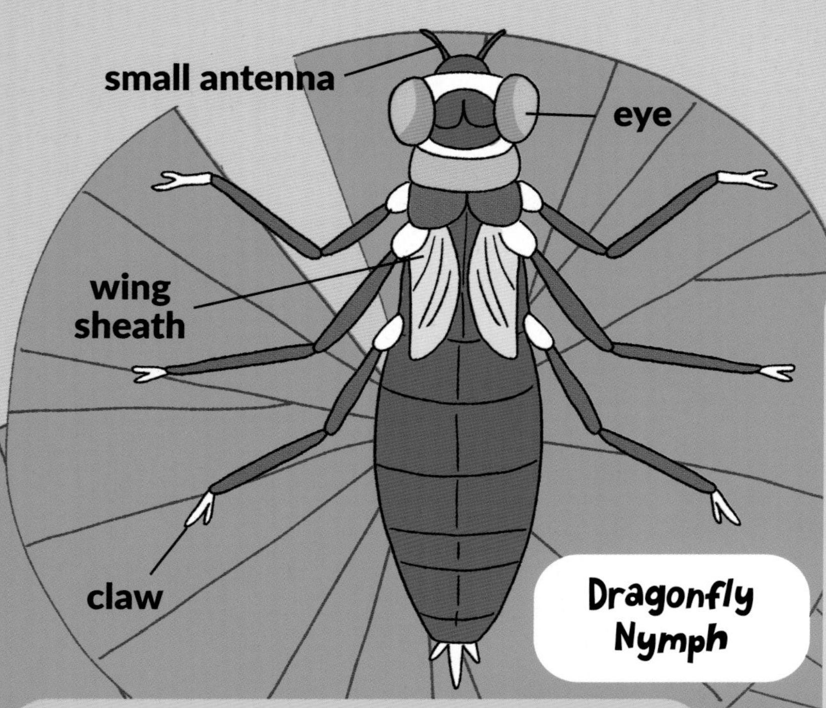

Dragonfly Nymph

In their larval stage, dragonflies live in water. During this stage of their life cycle, they are known as nymphs.

Dragonflies and damselflies both have **colourful bodies** and wings. They use their speed and agility to hunt.

Though dragonflies can't breathe fire like their namesakes!

When resting, the dragonfly **opens its wings**. The damselfly will keep them closed.

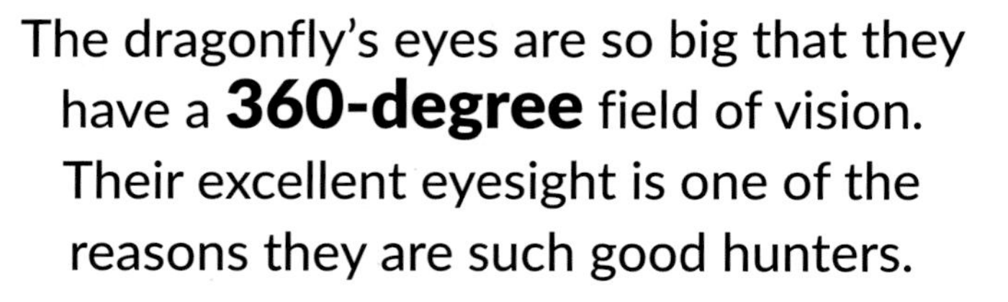

The dragonfly's eyes are so big that they have a **360-degree** field of vision. Their excellent eyesight is one of the reasons they are such good hunters.

It's hard to sneak past someone with eyes in the back of their head!

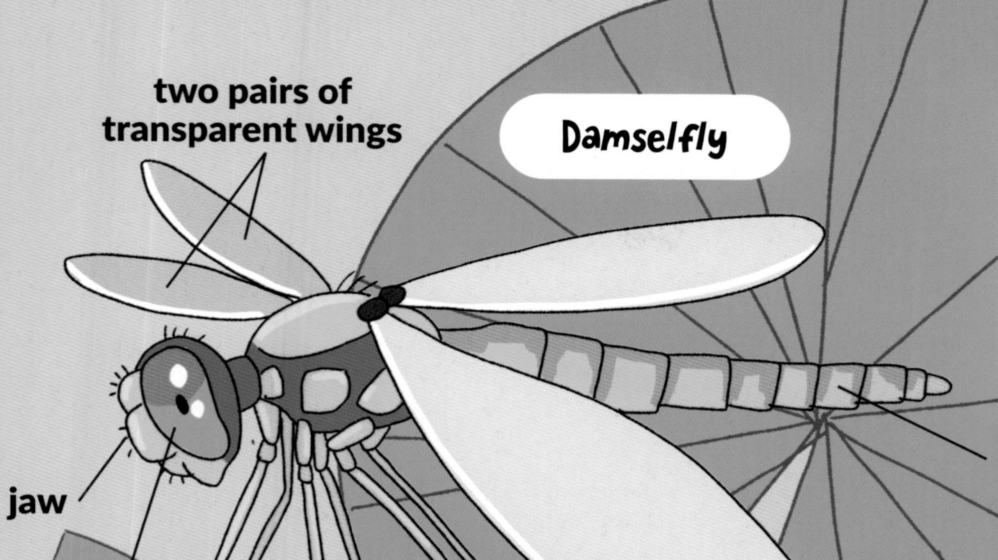

Dragonflies have some weird and funny nicknames including **devil's darning needle** and **snake doctor**.

The damselfly is slimmer and more **fragile** than the dragonfly.

An adult **dragonfly's wingspan** can be as great as 16cm (6in).

Dragonflies have been around for **300 million years** and some giant prehistoric species had wingspans of nearly 1m (3.3ft).

Now that sounds more like a real dragon!

Some dragonflies complete an **18,000km** (11,200mi) round-trip migration.

That's three times the distance from London to New York!

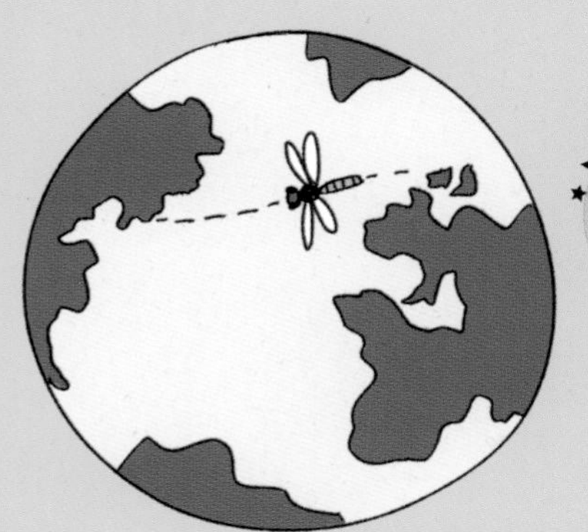

Neither damselflies nor dragonflies can use their legs for walking. They are simply used for **perching** when at rest or to catch prey when hunting.

Why walk when you can fly?

Wasps and Hornets

There are more than **100,000** types of wasp around the world.

very BIG number

Wasps make their nests by **chewing wood** into a paper-like substance and sticking it all together.

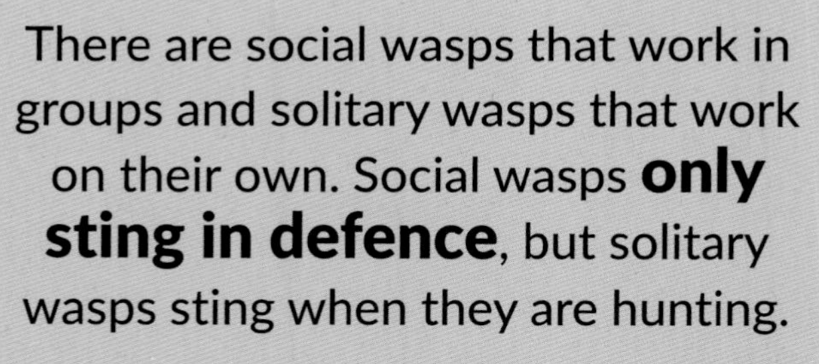

There are social wasps that work in groups and solitary wasps that work on their own. Social wasps **only sting in defence**, but solitary wasps sting when they are hunting.

Solitary wasps never get invited to the social wasps' parties.

Wasps are very useful for **controlling pests**.

No, we don't mean your parents!

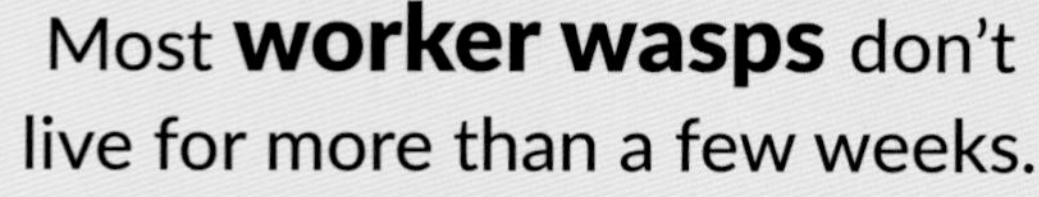

Most **worker wasps** don't live for more than a few weeks.

You probably wouldn't last long if you had to work as hard as they do!

What's the difference between a wasp and a hornet?

Hornets are actually just another type of wasp, but they tend to be much larger.

The Asian giant hornet is the **biggest wasp** at 4.5cm (1.8in) long.

In Japan, **hornets are eaten** as a delicacy.

BRAIN BURSTER

Hornet stings are **more painful** than other wasp stings due to their powerful venom.

A wasp nest found in Australia weighed **90kg** (198lb).

Which is, appropriately, the weight of a fully grown kangaroo!

Water Insects

Insects often live in water in the **early stages** of their lives. For example, dragonfly nymphs and mosquito larvae are both water-dwelling.

Some insects, such as the appropriately named **diving beetle**, live their whole lives in water.

Water insects have different ways to **breathe underwater**. Dragonfly nymphs have gills and mosquito larvae use snorkel-like breathing tubes.

Water striders (or pond skaters) live on top of ponds and pools. They are able to walk on the surface due to microscopic hairs on their legs that repel water.

Water insects are bugs that live a part of their **life cycle in water**.

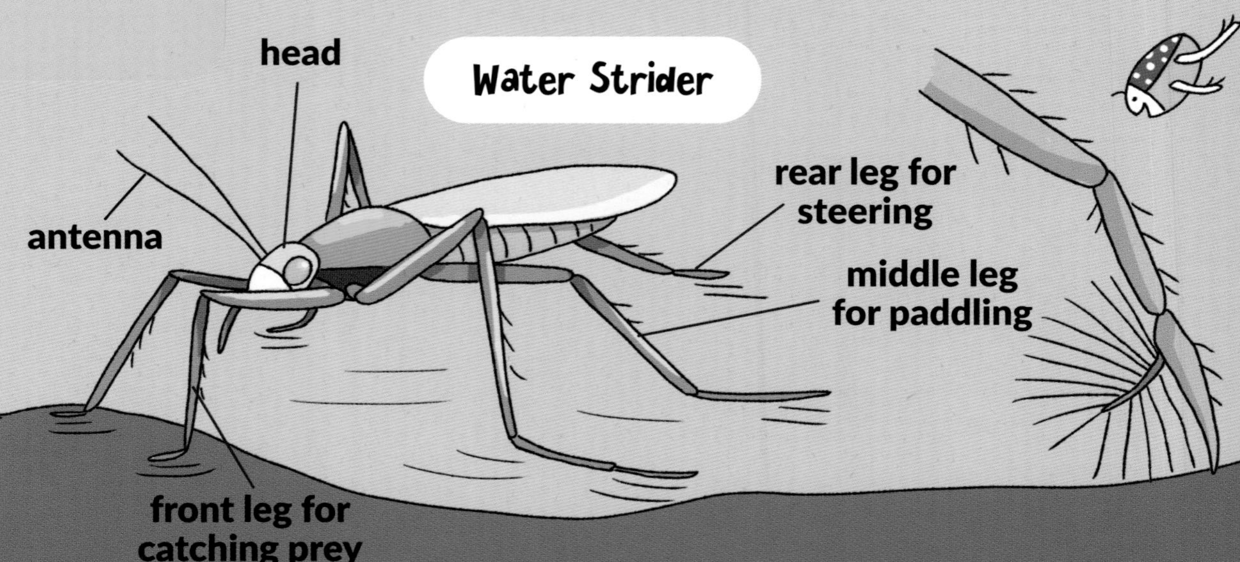

Water Bug
rear leg used for paddling or steering
large leg for catching prey
large flattened body
There are giant water bugs known as 'toe-biters' that have a very painful bite. They can be found in North and South America, northern Australia and East Asia.
Water insects break down dead things in freshwater rivers and lakes. This helps to keep the water clean.
THINK I MIGHT NEED TO CHANGE THE BAG!
Most water insects swim around, but mosquito larvae like to hang upside down from the surface of the water.
They are just trying to be as cool as vampire bats!
The diving beetle can attack fish that are significantly larger than itself.
WHAT ARE YOU LOOKING AT?
BRAIN BURSTER
Water striders are one of the few insects that survive in the ocean. Not many insects choose to make the sea their home.

Beetles and Weevils

very **BIG** number

Beetles are the largest group of insects on Earth with around **370,000** different types. Of those, 10% are weevils.

When do we get to the dung beetle?

Beetles often have beautiful, **brightly coloured** shells.

Beetles play an important part in keeping the natural world clean but some are pests. The elm bark beetle spreads **Dutch elm disease**, which kills elm trees.

Cleaning up, say, dung for example?

Okay, okay, everyone's favourite beetle is the **dung beetle**! It forms animal poo into balls which it rolls around as both a home and food source.

We love you, dung beetle!

Beetles live in lots of **different habitats**, from deserts to rainforests, and have varied diets to match.

Some might eat animal dung...

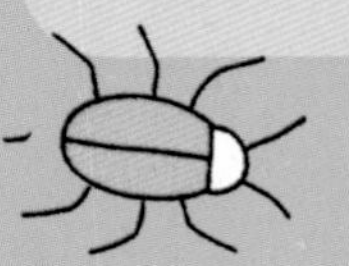

Beetles can grow to enormous sizes. A fully grown **goliath beetle** can weigh 100g (3.5oz) and the titan beetle from South America can reach almost 20cm (8in) in length.

The dung beetle is also the **strongest animal** in the world for its size, and it is able to push a load that's over a thousand times its own body weight.

BRAIN BURSTER

That's like an average man being able to push six double-decker buses at once!

Dung beetle, we salute you!

Weevils are sometimes known as **snout beetles** due to their unusually long noses.

Many weevils are **crop pests** and are named after the crops that they damage.

The scariest one is the chocolate weevil!

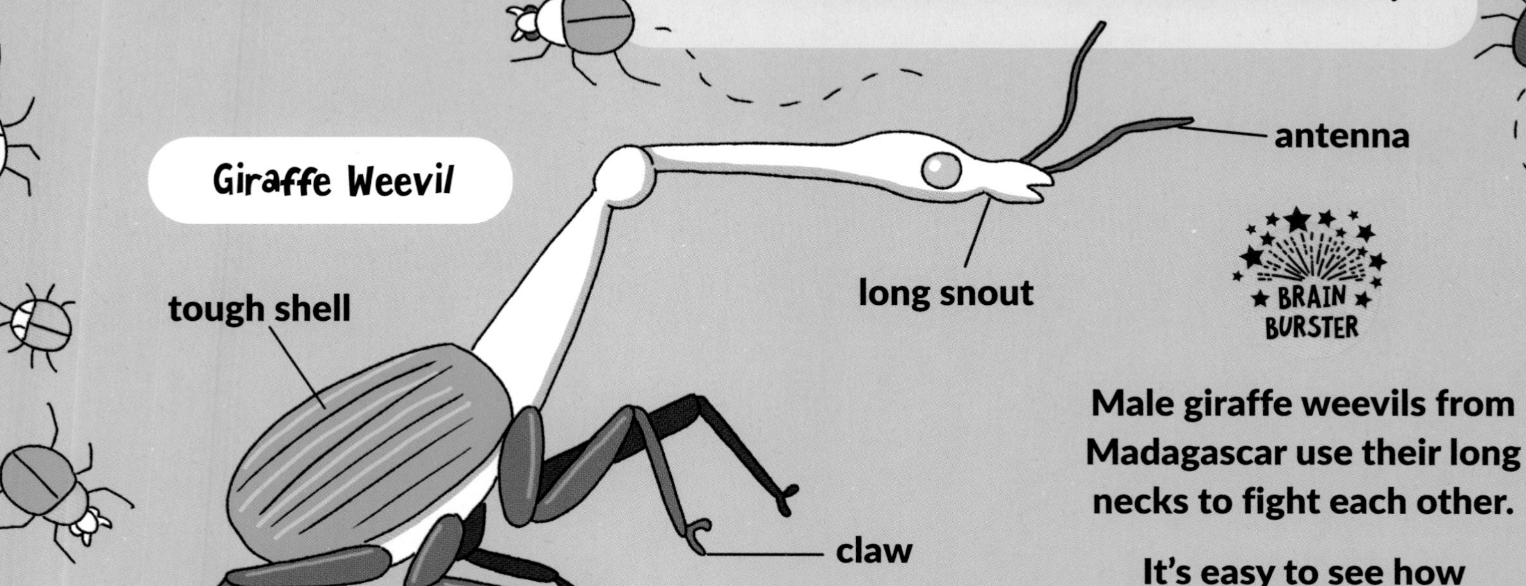

BRAIN BURSTER

Male giraffe weevils from Madagascar use their long necks to fight each other.

It's easy to see how they got their name!

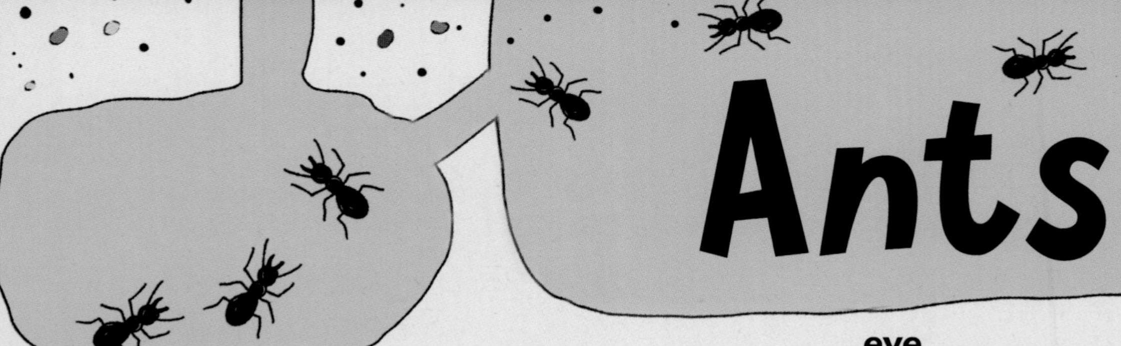

Ants

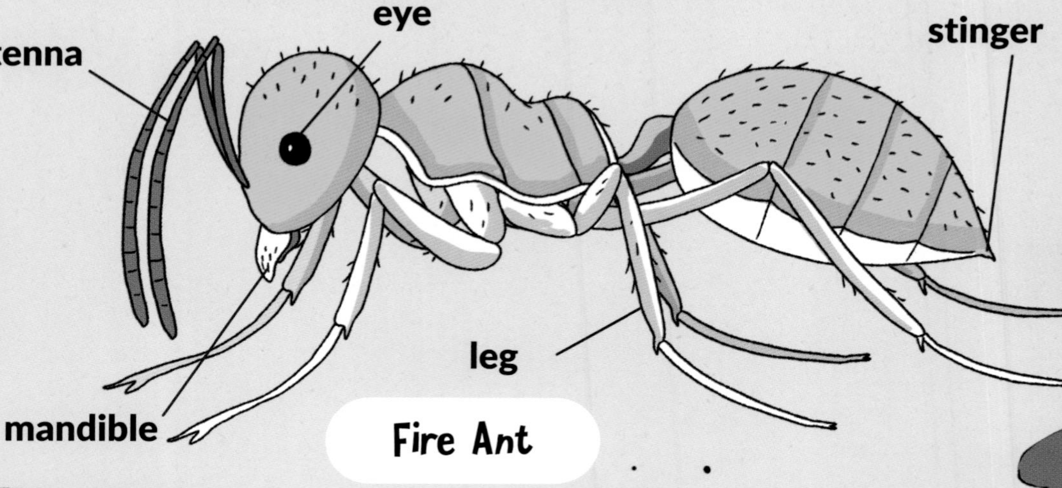

There are over **10,000 species** of ant. Ants live in groups called colonies.

Ants have **two sets of jaws** – one carries food or useful objects, the other is used just for eating.

I ALSO HAVE A THIRD, MUCH FANCIER SET OF JAWS, BUT I SAVE THOSE FOR SPECIAL OCCASIONS!

In a colony, there are **queen ants** who lay eggs, female worker ants, and male ants whose job is to mate with the queen.

Leafcutter ants compete with dung beetles in the strength stakes; they can lift up to **fifty times** their own body weight!

There are estimated to be ten quadrillion ants on Earth. That's **10,000,000,000,000,000**.

A single ant nest can easily contain over **100,000** ants.

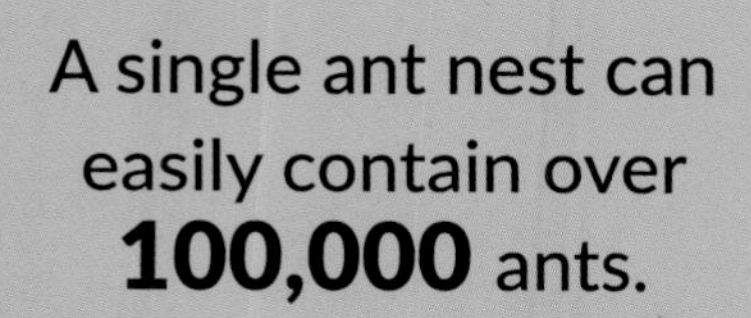

The highly aggressive **red fire ant** was accidentally imported to the United States. This species is now responsible for $3 billion worth of vet and medical bills ever year.

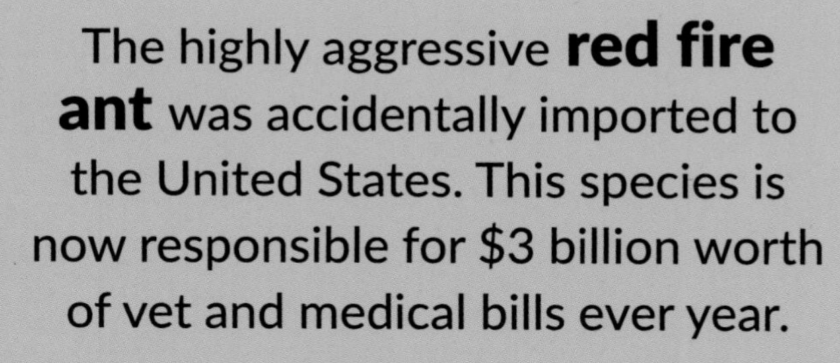

They sound quite ant-isocial.

BRAIN BURSTER

Fossil specimens show that some **prehistoric ants** were over 5cm (2in) long!

They must have been gi-ants!

Ants are not water insects, but they can **survive underwater** for considerable periods of time.

Army ants form **huge colonies** that are always on the move. They can kill and eat much larger animals, such as lizards, due to their vast numbers.

The queens of some ant colonies can live for up to **30 years**.

Does that make her an ant-ique?

Moths

Moths are **masters of stealth** with their dull wing patterns blending into the background to provide natural camouflage.

Moths use the Moon's light to navigate, so **artificial light** confuses their sense of direction. This is the reason moths flutter around lamps at night.

Moths are often regarded as pests and can be **harmful to crops**, but they also play an important role as pollinators.

Butterflies may be more colourful, but moths have the numbers. There are about **nine times more** moths in the world than butterflies.

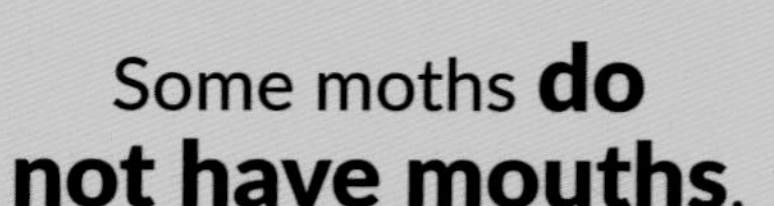

Some moths **do not have mouths**. They do not need to eat as they only live for a short time in order to mate.

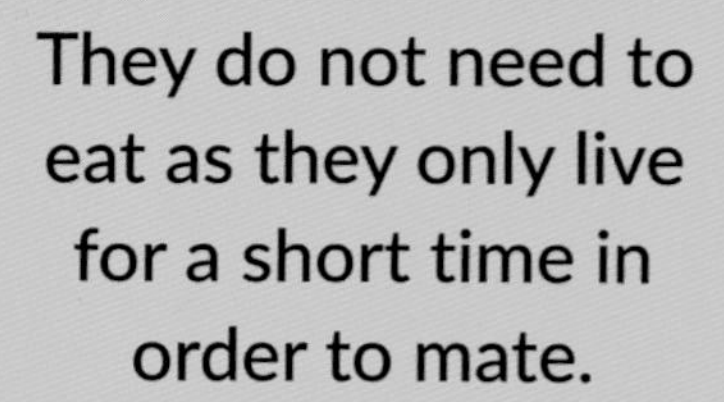

This also explains why you've never heard a moth singing.

The largest moth in the world is the atlas moth of Southeast Asia. Its wingspan can reach as much as 30cm (12in)!

Atlas Moth

antenna

wing

Moth's wings are incredibly **brittle** and can be broken very easily.

Bats love to eat moths, so tiger moths produce an **ultrasonic click** that confuses bats' senses.

BRAIN BURSTER

In 1947, a dead moth was removed from a computer at Harvard University. It had been causing a series of malfunctions, and so it was **an actual bug in one of the earliest computers**.

A male moth can **smell a female moth** from more than 6km (4mi) away.

Now that's what we call perfume!

Spiders

Spiders are not insects but belong to a group of creepy crawlies called **arachnids**, which also includes scorpions. Almost all arachnids have eight legs – two more than insects – and unlike insects, arachnids don't have wings or antennae.

This makes them much better jugglers!

The largest spiders are tarantulas and the biggest of them is the fearsome goliath tarantula, which has a 30cm (12in) leg span!

Webs are easily damaged, so spiders will often **rebuild their webs** every night. To do this, they produce over 20m (66ft) of silk.

Some spiders like their food gooey! They inject their prey with a liquid that **melts their insides** and then suck them dry!

Bet you're glad you're not a fly!

The trapdoor spider lives in a burrow covered by a 'door' made from soil and debris. When the spider feels the vibrations of an insect above, it jumps out to surprise its prey.

Spiders are natural insecticides; a single spider may eat **hundreds of small flies** every day!

very BIG number

There are over 40,000 species of spider. A study once found that one field of undisturbed grass contained over **five million spiders**!

Still feel like having a picnic?

BRAIN BURSTER

For its weight, **spider silk is tougher than steel** and Kevlar – the material used to make bulletproof vests!

Spiders produce up to **seven different types of silk** from a liquid stored inside them.

Stick and Leaf Insects

Stick and leaf insects are the true masters of disguise of the bug world. They use their natural resemblance to leaves and twigs to blend perfectly into the foliage.

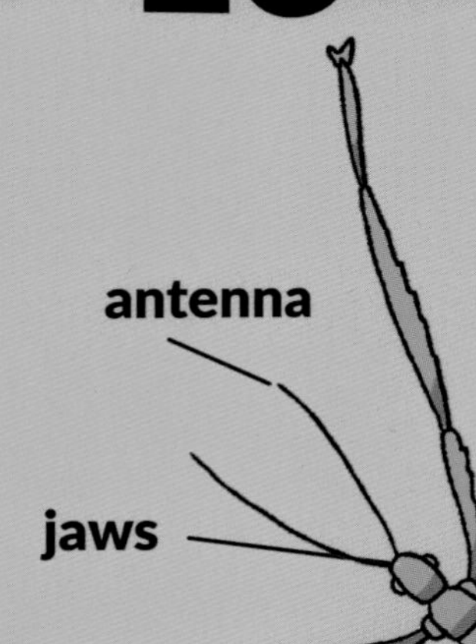

Stick insects vary hugely in length from a tiny 1.25cm (0.5in) to a **record-breaking 62cm** (24in).

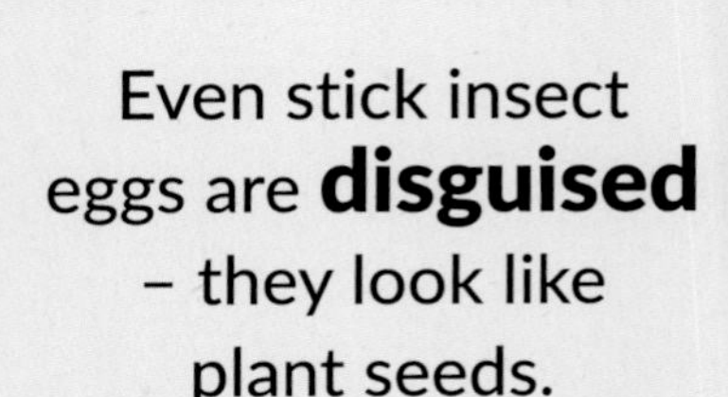

Even stick insect eggs are **disguised** – they look like plant seeds.

Stick insects are only **active at night**. During the day they stay completely motionless. This makes them even harder to spot!

It also makes them annoyingly good at musical statues!

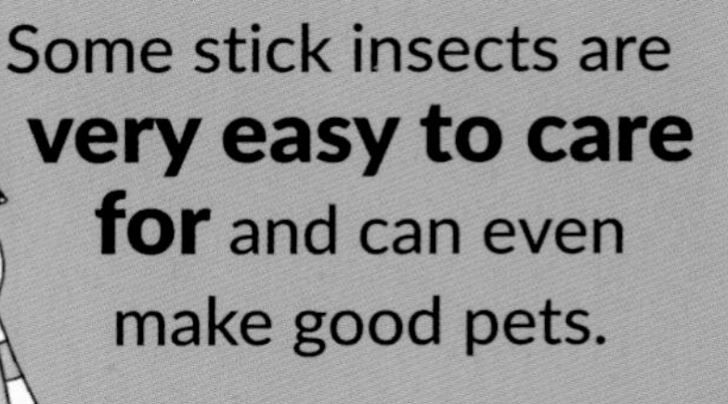

Some stick insects are **very easy to care for** and can even make good pets.

Though you can only take them for short walks.

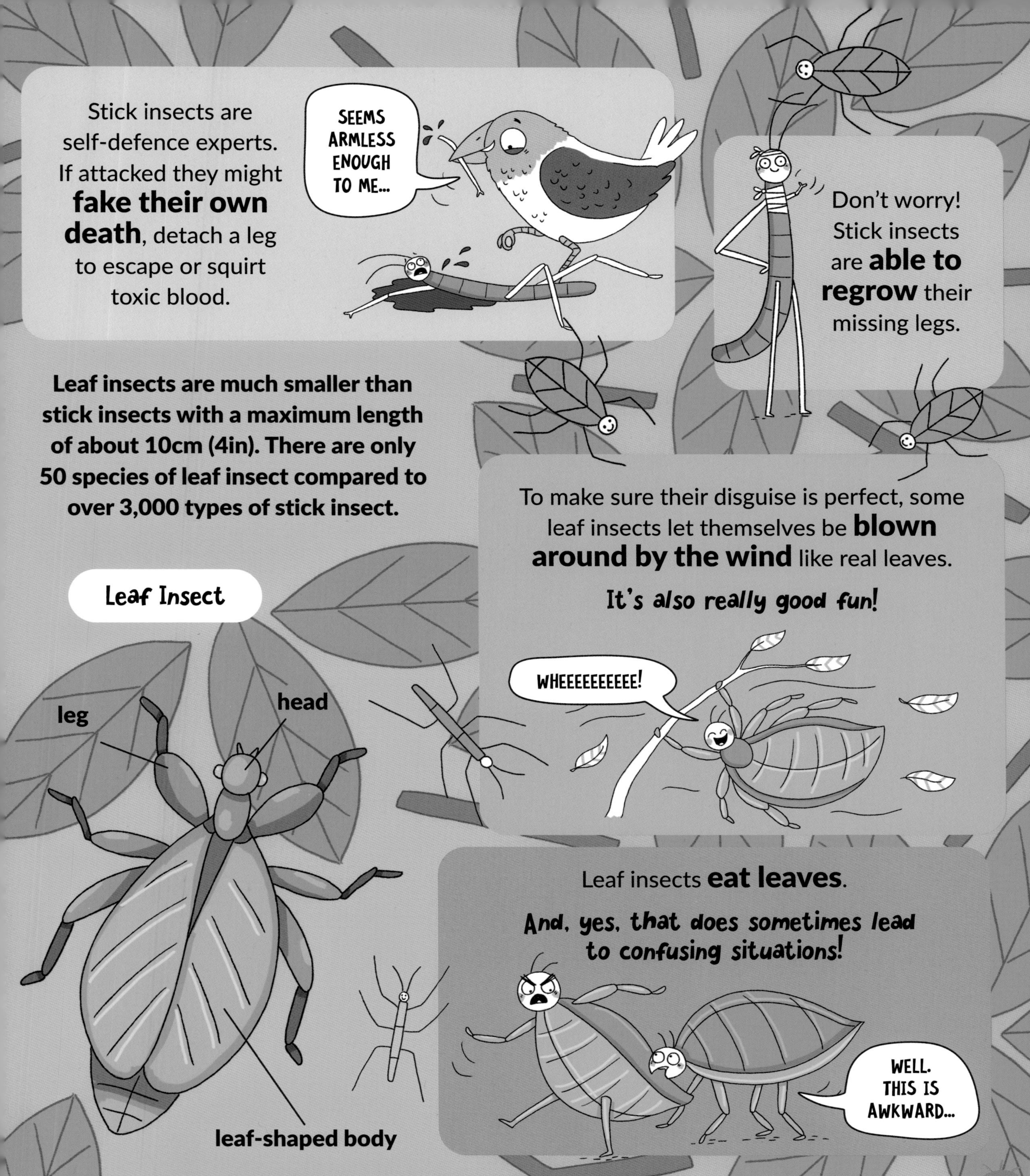
Stick insects are self-defence experts. If attacked they might **fake their own death**, detach a leg to escape or squirt toxic blood.
SEEMS ARMLESS ENOUGH TO ME...
Don't worry! Stick insects are **able to regrow** their missing legs.
Leaf insects are much smaller than stick insects with a maximum length of about 10cm (4in). There are only 50 species of leaf insect compared to over 3,000 types of stick insect.
To make sure their disguise is perfect, some leaf insects let themselves be **blown around by the wind** like real leaves.
It's *also* really good fun!
WHEEEEEEEEEE!
Leaf Insect
leg
head
leaf-shaped body
Leaf insects **eat leaves**.
And, yes, that does sometimes lead to confusing situations!
WELL. THIS IS AWKWARD...

TOP TEN Weird Bug Facts

10

The fastest running insect in the world is the tiny mite *Paratarsotomus macropalpis*, which can run at up to **322 body lengths per second**. That's like a human running at over 2,000kmph (1,200mph).

That's almost double the speed of sound!

9

A rocket with a cargo of fruit flies was **launched into space** on 20th February 1947. This meant that insects were the first living things sent into space.

8

Termite queens can live for up to **70 years**. Researchers have found that termites work faster when rock music is played.

7

Honeybees have **hairy** eyeballs!

6

Bombardier beetles can shoot **a jet of scalding chemicals** to protect themselves. These jets can reach 100°C (212°F) and cause nasty burns.

Ouch! That's the same temperature as boiling water!

5
Some ants can make themselves **explode** when they are attacked.
OOOH, SOMETIMES I GET SO ANGRY I COULD JUST EXPLODE!
4
Some fleas can jump more than 200 times their own height.
This would be like a person being able to jump over the Eiffel Tower.
THAT'S SOME HIGH JUMP!
3
All the **ants in the world** would weigh about the same as all the humans.
Just be glad that they're a lot smaller than us!
2
Dung beetles **use the stars** to navigate.
TAKE THE SECOND STAR ON THE RIGHT!
1
A cockroach can **survive for up to a week** without its head...
HAVE YOU LOST WEIGHT?

Fun Bug Activities

Draw the slimiest, hairiest, most outrageous creepy crawly that you can think of.

There are bonus points for extra eyes.

Here are some bug parts to inspire you!

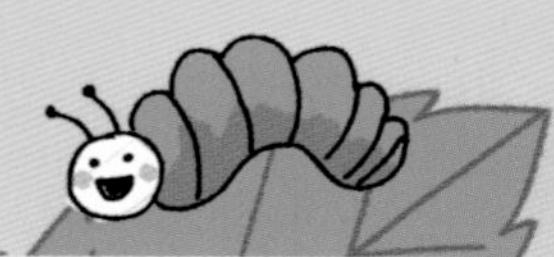

Go on a bug safari in the garden. Grab a camera and try to take photos of as many different bugs as you can.

Try competing with a friend to see who can find the most!

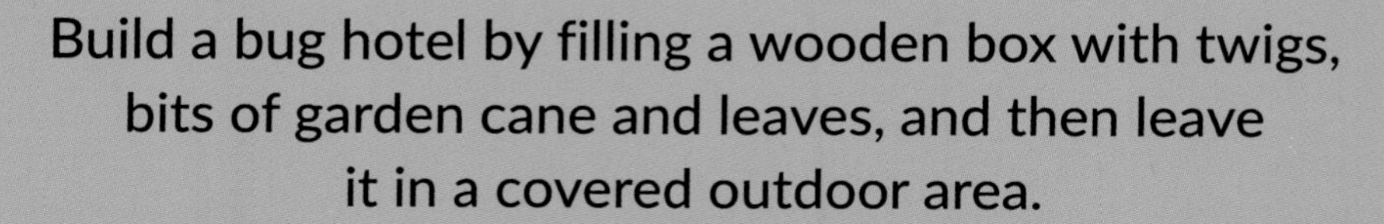

Build a bug hotel by filling a wooden box with twigs, bits of garden cane and leaves, and then leave it in a covered outdoor area.

Check back to see who might have moved in!

Let's Play Beetle!

Here's a fun insect game that you can play with your friends. All you need is some paper, some pencils and a dice! The aim of the game is to be the first player to finish a picture of a beetle.

The **youngest** player rolls the dice first. Each player then throws the dice in turn and draws **body parts** of their beetle depending on the number they rolled.

You must **draw** the body first, so you can't start until you **throw a six**. You must also roll a **five** to draw the **head** before you can add the eyes and antennae.

The dice rolls needed for each **body part** are as follows:

- Throw a **six** to draw the beetle's body
- Throw a **five** to draw the beetle's head
- Throw a **four** to draw each of the beetle's two wings
- Throw a **three** to draw each of the beetle's six legs
- Throw a **two** to draw each of the beetle's two antennae
- Throw a **one** to draw each of the beetle's two eyes

The first player to draw a complete beetle shouts **"BEETLE!"** and is the winner of that round.

Glossary

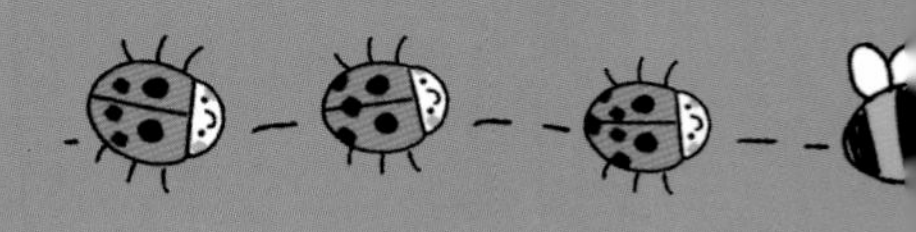

Abdomen The lower part of an insect's body, which contains the organs for digesting food and producing young.

Antenna Long, thin body part that sticks out from an insect's head and is used for sensing objects. Plural is antennae.

Arachnid A group of small eight-legged animals, which include spiders and scorpions.

Breed To produce young by mating.

Bug A type of insect with piercing and sucking mouthparts.

Carbon dioxide A gas in the air and one that people release when they breathe out.

Defence mechanism An animal's automatic response to protect itself.

Field of vision The whole area that an animal can see with its eyes in one fixed position.

Fossil The remains or trace of a living thing preserved in rock.

Gills Organs on the sides of fish and some other animals that live in water that enable them to breathe underwater.

Habitat The natural home of a living thing.

Insecticide A chemical used for killing insects.

Larva The worm-like young of an animal, which hatches from an egg and changes completely as it turns into an adult. Plural is larvae.

Migrate To go on a long journey to find a new home. Animals do this to find somewhere warmer to live or to breed.

Pollinate To take pollen from the male part of a flower to the female part so that plants can make seeds and reproduce.

Predator An animal that kills and eats other animals.

Prey An animal that is killed and eaten by another animal.

Proboscis The long, sucking mouthpart of an insect used for feeding.

Pupa A larva, often motionless and wrapped up in a hard covering, which is changing into an adult. Plural is pupae.

Regurgitate To bring back swallowed food to the mouth.

Species A group of animals or plants that have similar characteristics.

Stealth Quiet and secretive behaviour.

Thorax The section of an insect's body between the head and the abdomen.

Toxic Poisonous and harmful.

Ultrasonic Using sound waves higher than humans can hear.

Wingspan The distance from the end of one wing (in a pair) to the end of the other.